FANTASTIC BEASTS

AND WHERE TO FIND TH

FIGHTING MODERN EVILS
FANTASTIC BEASTS AND WHERE TO FIND THEM

MUGGLE WORTHY

FANTASTIC BEASTS AND WHERE TO FIND THEM

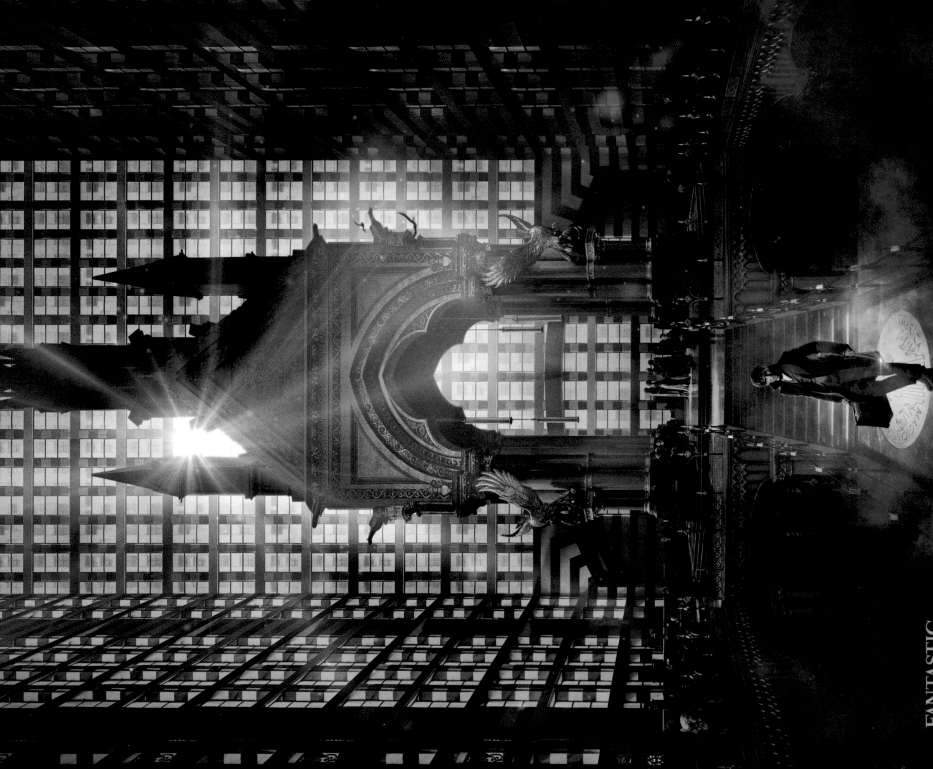

FANTASTIC
BEASTS
AND WHERE
TO FIND THEM

FANTASTIC
BEASTS

™ & © WBEI

STUPEFY

FANTASTIC
BEASTS
AND WHERE
TO FIND THEM

™ & © WBEI

Fly to New York for...
...a Broom with a View
New York
London
FOR POSTAGE
FANTASTIC BEASTS AND WHERE TO FIND THEM
TM & © WBEI